The Body, Beauty, and Bravery Project

The Body, Beauty, and Bravery Project

A Five Week Study of What's Really True About Your Body

Alison Cross MS, LPC, CPCS

ISBN: 1546988696
ISBN-13: 9781546988694

DEDICATED TO MY FAMILY, ESPECIALLY MY GIRLS

Contents

Acknowledgments

I started writing this book about 10 years ago. It's had many different versions and I finally printed up my own copies and sold nearly all of them in my workshops and through my private practice. Even though I felt for the most part that I had checked this box I never felt at peace about what I produced. It felt that I needed to return to this idea because it wasn't finished yet. Many years passed and in my practice one day a woman walked into her first appointment with me. As her story unravels she pulls out a copy of my book and I was shocked. I hadn't met this woman before but a dear friend had given her a copy and it had made a difference in her life. She began to question her lifelong obsession with food and body image. She was ready to work on what drove her here in the first place, the real emotional and spiritual issues that we all have but get distracted from because of our hyper focus on what we choose to put into our mouths. That was my first nudge from the Holy Spirit in a long time to start again on this project. What would make it accessible to more people? As I pondered this question another nudge came my way. In my Monday night women's Bible study I discovered the beauty of short weekly studies that were simple but packed a punch. Imagining my book in this format excited me, especially since it allows so much room for the Spirit to work on each reader and each group as He sees fit. I know, He does that regardless, but this style really worked for me, a very busy Mom whose mind often tracks many details daily. I'm guessing this format will work the same for other women who are also busy and important. Thank you Lisa Sweeting, Renee Horne, Elizabeth Harper, Stacy Abston, Chris Shaw, my Monday night Ladies, the Gorgeous Woman from my office, Colleagues, my Parents, Bill & Lynda Scaggs, my Husband, Ian who's had more conversations about body image than an average suburban Dad, and my girls, Avary, Lily, Shannon, and Jillian who inspire me daily to show up and be heard.

Introduction

This book was written for women who have a relationship with Jesus Christ, and who also happen to desire a better body image. In church and in relationships with other Christians we learn more about God and how to be like Him. But the subject of body image rarely comes up, except to complain about ourselves in some way. The Bible is very clear, however, in what our attitudes should be concerning our physical beings, "I am fearfully and wonderfully made, ...I know that full well" (Psalm 139:14). If you've picked up this book, maybe you're already curious about how all this negative language affects you and others around you. Perhaps the Spirit is already developing an awareness of the fact that something's wrong. Where did this language come from? How is it a part of Christian culture? Here's a personal question for you: Could body shaming be holding you back spiritually, from fully embracing the love and complete acceptance that God has for you?

Well, for one thing, if you are feeling physically "less than," you sound just like everybody else. I remember one morning at my gym in the locker room where a young woman looked in the mirror and proclaimed, "There's nothing about myself that I like." And this coming from a former Miss America contestant! OK, not really, but that was believable wasn't it? Because we're not strangers to body hatred. It's something that all women experience *and have grown comfortable with*. Sadly, there's nothing about us that distinguishes us from non-believers. It's as if we didn't see ourselves the way God sees us.

Because we don't.

The Bible has answers for you and offers you something very different than the captivity of today's beauty standards (and resulting body negativity). It is my belief that we are all beautiful, inside and out. The diversity that comes with body type, skin color, cultural influences, and age differences-there's beauty in all of it. Yes, God cares about our hearts the most. But what we're failing to claim is joy, appreciation, and yes, amusement at our physical appearance. It's not meant to be our only focus in life, nor the way in which we get people to like or approve of us. To choose a mindset based on the Bible means to go against the "basic principles of this world" (Colossians 2:8). It means to embrace our beauty inside and out, and apply bravery in our daily lives to keep living this way. Why bravery? Because you'd be making a conscious effort to be different in this cultural climate. You'd be loving your body!

This five- week journey is comprised of a weekly story (**body**), a Bible verse to memorize and meditate upon (**beauty**), and the opportunity to practice a positive body image in your daily life (**bravery**). I ask a lot of questions in the bravery section, so you may want to keep a journal handy to record your thoughts. Be prepared with an open spirit as you embrace what God would have for you here. Having a great body image is in direct contradiction to our culture, and in total violation of the captivity the enemy would like to keep you in. Know that this will be a battle, and I will be praying for you! It takes real bravery to reject the negativity and to embrace the diversity of beauty that you see in yourself and others. Staying connected with a group of women and taking this journey together definitely helps, especially if there's a group of friends that you're already practicing vulnerability with. Encouragement and accountability are essential. So grab your Bible, and let's go!

And the goal is, of course, to *live beautiful, live brave*.

"I love my body."

Body: The Truth

I love my body. I say that as an affirmation, and for the most part, I believe it. My feminine existence in this culture depends on it if I am to stay strong. My ability to lead as a parent of 4 daughters depends on it. My relationship with my husband benefits from it. And my role as a leader in the community for women and girls depends on it. Say it out loud, won't you? *I love my body.*

Others may whisper and tear it down. I don't stay at the gym all day, haven't paid for beauty/medical procedures, and unless they try to kill me (ie cancer) then my boobs will remain "real." I don't join in when other women complain about their legs, butt, or mushroomy waist. I tolerate the moment when the aerobics instructor shouts out how many calories we're burning. I roll my eyes when I hear "if you don't squeeze it, no one will!" As if my beauty and body acceptance depends on how much I work out, or depends on what a loved one thinks of my body.

Almost every message around us says that we should look different than we really are. And we're listening. $11.8 billion dollars were spent on cosmetic surgeries in 2008-I quote from this time period because that was the same year we had a huge economic decline. But manifesting control over our outer beauty stayed strong. Every teen group that I talk to, regardless of economic and cultural backgrounds, agree that a size 0 is ideal. Jean Kilbourne in her documentary "Killing Us Softly, Part 4"[1] says that in our time, "...literally our girls aspire to be nothing." Negative comparisons amongst women are rampant ("I wish I had her abs/butt/legs, etc."). I couldn't even tell you the last time I heard a woman say something good about herself.

To be successful in loving your body, you must start right now. Even if there are healthy, positive changes you'd like to make (and you just consumed a box of cookies), *it's vital to your wellbeing to love yourself, perceived flaws and all.*

Beauty: Psalms 139:14 "I praise you because I am fearfully and wonderfully made; your works are wonderful, I know that full well."

Bravery:
Day 1: Take a few deep breaths. I like to open each moment that you're working on this with breath work. If you're like me, you could be taking care of this quickly like a task. Deep breaths slow your mind and make you focus on your physical presence in the moment. It literally reprograms your brain and gives you an opportunity to focus. Check in with how you feel right now. We carry a lot of tension and emotion from moment to moment and part of body acceptance is being able to interpret what's going on in your body. Is it just tension? What emotion is affecting your body? What thoughts are running through your head as a reaction to the meditation above? Use the space below to record some thoughts.

_____

_____

_____

_____

Think of your body as it is right now. What do you enjoy about it? If you're having difficulty, have you really considered all the details of what makes up your physical being? God doesn't play favorites. He says it right there in the verse, you are "fearfully and wonderfully made." There's no footnote or statistic stating that only covers a certain percentage of us! So, with an open spirit and no judgment, what do you like/love/enjoy?

_____

_____

Go to God now with your list, and repeat the verse to Him. Sit in silence, breathing deeply, knowing that your God loves each part of you like crazy, and authored the diversity and beauty in the world around us, and in your mirror.

~~

Psalms 139:14 "I praise you because I am fearfully and wonderfully made; your works are wonderful, I know that full well."

~~

Record an affirmative statement about yourself. (Examples: I'm working on my body image and I won't hate myself forever, I love my toes, I enjoy my laugh, my body tells my story, etc.) Maybe you also have some thoughts to record from your time with Him. Write them here.

_____
_____
_____
_____
_____
_____

Day 2: Hello Beautiful! Are you ready for more brave steps in loving your body? Let's get ready. Take a few deep breaths. Check in with how you feel right now emotionally and record it here:

_____

What stands in your way to loving your body? What are some of the negative thoughts and judgments you have specifically? Have you ever said them out loud to God? Go ahead. Give him the riot act as if you were speaking to someone from Customer Service. I'll give you a moment. Or, if you're in a public place, maybe just write them down...

_____

_____

_____

_____

_____

_____

_____

Now, how did that make you feel? (I'm a therapist, I have to ask that, and yes, you really need to record it here):

_____

Imagine God taking your list of complaints-your negative thoughts and beliefs-and replacing them with light. Take a few minutes, breathing and imagining this happen, the light flowing all around your body. This light is made up of love and truth, and you weren't meant to walk around with these negative thoughts in your head. Instead you're meant to walk with meaning, purpose, and confidence that ALL of you matters to Him and is lovely.

Let's pretend that you were passed on directly to the CEO-God Himself. How would He handle your call? With yelling and anger? Does He care? Or is His compassion and understanding coming through?

Finally, repeat the verse of the week out loud.

~◡

"I praise you because I am fearfully and wonderfully made; your works are wonderful, I know that full well."

~◡

Record an affirmative statement about yourself here. Something you might say is, "I am loved." If there are more thoughts or feelings from your meditation above, please take the time and record them.

_____

_____

_____

_____

Day 3: Hello, you gorgeous lady! Take a few deep breaths. During your breath work, do a body scan. What are you bringing into this time today, physically and/or emotionally? List these things here:

_____

_____

Feeling fat today? Ever notice how much women say that? What in the world does that mean? How can I actually *feel* fat emotionally? Often our physical preoccupations are a cover up for uncomfortable emotions. Whenever I'm locked in on body negativity, I see it as a sign that I need to Find Another Thought (FAT-get it??) The way God values us inside and out is so powerful and we cut ourselves down to size when we only focus on the physical. Recognize a negative body image feeling as a signal that we need to go deeper and be real with ourselves about the real status of our heart in the moment.

Record an affirmative statement about yourself below. (For example, I choose to not feel guilty when I eat what I want, I am important enough to acknowledge my feelings, I refuse to give in to fat and ugly attacks, etc.)

_____

_____

Day 4: You are amazing! I'm so thankful you're here to check in. Let's do the breath work! Take a few deep breaths. Check in with how you feel right now, both physically and then emotionally:

_____

_____

"I praise you…" is how our verse starts off this week. Do you? I remember the day when my first daughter discovered her toes. That was probably one of the best days of her life! She was so proud of herself, and truly they amused her for a good long time. I still remember her smiles, her joy, and her laugh. When is the last time you really felt appreciative of a body part? We're not adorable babies anymore, but when did we lose the delight and start focusing on the number on the scale? Oh, that number! It's so disconnected from our worth. Did it *ever* challenge you to body positive bravery? I can't think of a bigger way to close our spirits to the lovely feeling of delight.

Have an open spirit as you record 3 things that you can take delight in physically and why. Want to be challenged? Start with the body part you hate the most.

_____
_____
_____
_____
_____
_____
_____

Day 5: Valuable and worthy Child of God! You have arrived at Day 5! You are rocking this. Now, take a few deep breaths. Check in with how you feel right now, both physically and then emotionally.

_____

_____

"I know that full well." Talk about an affirmative statement! Wholeheartedly the Psalmist knows his body is amazing and was created by the great I AM (Exodus 3:14). Close your eyes if you like and imagine yourself in His presence. Feel the warmth of his gaze as He takes you in. The Lord cares for your heart more than anything. Feel his hands direct your eyes away from your body image hang ups (do you feel how petty they are in His sight?) as He holds you in His warm embrace. Ask your Father to heal the pain of negative thoughts and to refresh truth and love into your life. You are His beloved, He will do this for you.

Look up I John 4:8. Do you think this could be applied to body image? Why or why not?

_____

_____

_____

_____

Look at Hosea 3:1. God's love is steadfast even though we routinely turn away. We are still trying to earn our own way in this life. Getting caught up in the cultural milieu of body negative thoughts, or *unnecessarily over-restricting food choices because "it's good for us" is substituting a new morality where we don't need one. I realize this is challenging because when it comes to food, boy is this personal! But that's exactly what this is. Body love is as personal as it gets.

Now look at Hosea 10:12:

"Sow righteousness for yourselves, reap the fruit of unfailing love, and break up your unplowed ground; for it is time to seek the Lord until He comes and showers His righteousness on you."

This verse is one of my favorites and has always challenged me. For me, it's about Christian daily living, being loved, and the hint to keep on working on my heart. What hardness is there that needs to be "plowed?" Could it be your body image? Is it possible that this could be healed as we seek God through this process?

Please know that I'm not trivializing anyone's experience with an eating disorder, disordered eating, or one's weight loss journey. These subjects are tough and complicated. My point is that we've

7

all been there, making choices that may have been extreme and/or unnecessary. For example, anyone ever substitute a diet milkshake in place of a regular lunch? So much energy and thought goes into our choices and it's simply too much-we've overthinking it and often there are other issues making these decisions complicated.

Journaling this week is highly recommended. I'm resisting structuring your time too much because a lot of this study is about opening up your heart to the direction that the Spirit is calling you to go! Journaling and talking these issues through with a trusted someone could potentially help you learn new ideas about yourself.

_____
_____
_____
_____
_____
_____
_____
_____
_____
_____
_____
_____
_____

Weekly Wrap-Up:

1. My body image is stronger this week because…

_____
_____
_____
_____

2. The issues that came up for me this week were:

_____

_____

_____

_____

3. What I did to seek understanding: (ie pray, talk to a friend,   read a body image book)

_____

_____

_____

_____

4. What did I learn about myself this week?

_____

_____

_____

5. What did I learn about God this week?

_____

_____

_____

"Sister, you don't need to change your body, you just need to change your perspective."

Week 2

Body: The Truth, part 2

When I wake up and get dressed every day, my eyes used to zero in on the same place-my belly. My bathroom mirror only reflects from the hips up, so besides my face I examine my zero-pack. I've noticed all along that it was bigger than other kids' bellies growing up. I never felt bad about it until I was openly criticized by peers off and on through childhood. I even remember a friend that I overheard telling someone else that I'd be a really cute girl if it weren't for my poochy stomach. Ahhhhh, the love! But I've since put a lot of these comments into perspective. It's taken me years but I finally realized all the energy that it took to hate my body could slowly and surely be targeted in another direction. Body hatred is a learned behavior that can be unlearned.

One thing you can do differently is to start feeling gratitude for your body. When you wake up and zero in on a body part that makes you feel bad about yourself, get some perspective. See your body and yourself as a whole human being. Our culture teaches us to break ourselves down into parts, parts that we can manipulate and control into what we'd prefer them to look like. A negative body image reflects a victim mentality, one where there's no hope and no real solution. Sister, you don't need to change your body, *you just need to change your perspective.*

Once you allow yourself to show gratitude for the body you've been given, take the blinders off so you can continually see your beauty, and that of others. The diversity of beauty is all around and it will astound you. **YOU** are a part of that. We can no longer wait around for men, other women, the beauty, fashion, or diet industries to give us this message. Your worth doesn't depend on your size or "goal weight." Take this truth for yourself-it's been there all along. You are already beautiful.

Beauty: Ephesians 5:1-2 "Follow God's example, therefore, as dearly loved children and walk in the way of love, just as Christ loved us and gave himself up for us as a fragrant offering and sacrifice to God."

Bravery:

Day 1: Woo Hoo! Week 2! You are such an amazing, beautiful, and brave woman to keep on digging into this worthy subject-your positive body image. Now, just like last time, take a few deep breaths. Check in with how you feel right now, both physically and then emotionally.

_____

_____

_____

Seeing yourself as a whole human being is a lot harder than you think. Women are typically objectified not just through media, but we were considered property for almost all of time. For generations seeing ourselves as "less than" has been the status quo. Our power has been limited to our outward appearance and ways we can manipulate it. Beginning to see ourselves as a whole starts with the simple things, like a check in for your physical and emotional well-being. We don't have to limit ourselves to these private sessions of judgment in our bathroom mirrors, and then let that sum up how our day is going to be. This is a hard habit to break but it doesn't have to dominate your soul. You still have the power to act on your own behalf.

You are a dearly loved child. This is your affirmative statement for today. Remind yourself that you are dearly loved.

Day 2: Hello, beautiful and lovely woman! What a worthy choice you are making in spending a few moments today on you. Let's get started! Take a few deep breaths. Check in with how you feel right now, both physically and then emotionally.

_____

_____

_____

When I ask women and girls what they like about their bodies, they respond with a small list usually. That's pretty good, I'm glad they like something. But the body image problems fester when we can only focus on the "bad parts." Obsessions can become so powerful that we cease to see the whole picture. We may even stop listening to reason and stop appreciating the whole perspective. We feel so far from appreciating the whole body that it can't even be visualized.

Dearly loved child, what are you really hung up on? The image of the perfectly toned abs, derriere or legs? Or just the idea of control over those things? How much time is taken up by your obsessions? Confess, dear Sister, but please don't waste your time on shame. Instead, visualize your change (not your "after" picture, your "inner" picture). Picture in your mind walking along in your life, in your skin, with determination in your heart and your mind living freely as you go through life. Nothing and no one defines your beauty today. Maybe walking around with the knowledge that you are loved, and have a connection to God through the Holy Spirit gives you the strength to do this: *BE your affirmation today!* Experiment as if you already have a great body image and see what happens. If you're still pondering what your negative body image vibes are all about, talk to someone! Get out of your head and be honest. Or use some journal time here:

_____

_____

_____

_____

_____

_____

_____
_____

Record an affirmative statement about yourself in your journal. Perhaps you could say something like, "I am wonderfully made," "I am curvy and gorgeous," or "I am connected to God, the author of my beauty."

_____
_____
_____

Day 3: You are such a rock star! I wish I could hear in person how your day went. But before we get started, let's take a few deep breaths. Check in with how you feel right now, both physically and then emotionally.

_____
_____
_____

How did it go yesterday, pretending you already had a great body image? What did that look like for you? What did you notice that was different than normal?

_____
_____
_____
_____

Our "beauty" verse this week refers to following Christ's example of not just being His dearly loved child, but to "walk in the way of love." His "walk" ended up in a sacrifice that restored our relationship to God. This walk was *His loving choice* because He was committed to the result. What do we need to shed, to sacrifice, to walk more in love? Our "result" is this journey towards accepting our bodies. So please remember Sister, no guilt or shame is allowed here. Just be curious and kind as you

work through this. See yourself in God's loving light, His dearly loved child, and wonder... *what could be different in your life? How could you walk with more love?* Our goal is freedom and more connection with ourselves and our loving Savior. What loving choices do you need to make for yourself? (If you're scared to voice it, it probably means it's something you most need to do. Be BRAVE and tell one person.) Journal your thoughts.

_____
_____
_____
_____
_____
_____
_____
_____

Record an affirmative statement about yourself in your journal. You could say something like, "I am a brave woman," or "I will not feel guilty about pondering self-love."

_____
_____
_____

Day 4: Greetings, fellow Warrior! Take a few deep breaths. Check in with how you feel right now, both physically and then emotionally.

_____
_____
_____

How's your spirit so far in this journey? Have you observed new feelings or beliefs in your life? Have you gotten to know yourself a bit better? How far are you willing to go with this? I hope you're ready, because I'd like to jump in and challenge you MORE.

Remember our verse for the week? Let's take a look at it again.

~⁓

Ephesians 5:1-2 "Follow God's example, therefore, as dearly loved children and walk in the way of love, just as Christ loved us and gave himself up for us as a fragrant offering and sacrifice to God."

~⁓

Christ didn't just give Himself as an offering, He was a "fragrant" offering. He was a sacrifice, and by tradition, sacrifices were given to express gratitude for worldly blessings received by God. I'm curious how body image fits into this. I believe we can see our bodies as a worldly blessing. It's the physical package that allows us to be in this world and experience God's beauty here. We get to be human! When we're wrapped up in our body shame, there's not much time to be in the world and enjoying it authentically. We're holding back our voices, hiding ourselves because we feel that physically we're not enough. How can we offer ourselves in love to others if we can't even love ourselves by being comfortable in our own skin?

The kind of personal rejection that shines through with a negative body image has very deep roots in our souls. It's hard to get this out of our system! But, *do you really want to let it go?* How challenging would it be for you to be your authentic self, belly fat and all, in this world? I'm asking you to give up something that may have been serving you somehow. Perhaps not feeling physically worthy has felt safe and the amount of "risks" you take to be yourself are comfortably minimal. How often do we try and get away with the least bit of sacrifice, when what we're giving up isn't helping us to walk like "dearly loved children?" There's something valuable there for you when you hold onto the negativity. *What is it?* How does body negativity work for you and help you feel more in control?

_____
_____
_____
_____

Take these thoughts before God. I'm curious what it would be like if you took your revelations and compared it with others you feel safe with. Sometimes it's hard to do this on your own, but if you're in a group you have the power of community. It's harder for lies to corrupt the power in the room if you feel supported and are willing to be vulnerable.

When you walk away today, be sure you've affirmed yourself as God's dearly loved child. You haven't lost that status, and it's important to know you are accepted and loved no matter what, even if you don't feel ready to make this sacrifice. Take at least 1 minute reflecting on this truth without distraction. 60...59....58...

Record an affirmative statement about yourself in your journal. Try, "No matter where I'm at with my body image, I know my God loves me and takes care of me." OR "I'm ready to be my authentic self." Either one or something in between is lovely and acceptable. Honor where you are truthfully at.

_____
_____
_____
_____
_____

Day 5: You are a beautiful woman, inside and out. Take some deep breaths, Lady! Check in with how you feel right now, both physically and then emotionally, and let's wrap this week up.

_____
_____
_____

Our "body" for the week contained this quote: "A negative body image reflects a victim mentality, one where there's no hope and no real solution. Sister, you don't need to change your body, *you just need to change your perspective."*

Did you ever think of yourself as a victim? What have been your successes in life? We probably do a fairly decent job of keeping up appearances. Perhaps having body negativity is part of that...but should we strive to fit in that way? (The answer is "no.")

When I've been hurt and I'm down for the count, part of me wants to stay down and acknowledge the punches. They hurt, and I was (figuratively) struck down. I want the world to see how much this moment sucks for me and receive whatever validation and encouragement I can from that. But staying there for long is NOT an option. Nothing changes there, and God isn't honored there. I can't get on with my life, and ultimately all of me can't be ME if I stay.

Another example of victim mentality is our hang up with size. I see all around me women and girls who are enslaved by a NUMBER. It's that dang goal weight or dress size!! How much does that number victimize you and keep you holding onto your negative body image?? I know you want to be healthy, but who gave you that number in the first place? Was it a time in your life that you felt everything was going great? Or maybe someone was selling you something and felt with the proper controls, you can get anything you want, including this number.

Walking in the way of love may mean giving up the power that these numbers have over you. You are dearly loved, which means you're not alone.

Weekly Wrap-Up:

1. My body image is stronger this week because…

_____
_____
_____
_____

2. How did you feel about your affirmative statements this week? If you felt disconnected from what you wrote, perhaps you should post reminders of your affirmation on your mirror? You could also set it as a reminder on your phone, create a bookmark, or post it in your car. All day long, you are beautiful.

_____
_____
_____
_____

3. Did you feel the Spirit going deeper this week? What did you find yourself pondering over?

_____
_____
_____
_____

4. Look at Ephesians 1:15-23. What a beautiful prayer of thanksgiving! Did the Spirit of revelation and wisdom come over you this week? What did you learn about yourself that was new?

_____
_____
_____
_____

5. This week we talked about being a dearly loved child of God. Children are natural imitators of their parents. Taking on this role, we're looking to Christ as the Way and the Life that we can choose to follow. Were there any issues that came up for this week that would prevent you from following this path of self- love?

_____
_____
_____
_____

"Our comparisons can fuel obsessions about our bodies and their need to measure up. It's a vicious cycle that wears you out and only pretends to give you power."

Week 3

Body: The Body of My Dreams

re your dreams associated with a particular body type? What would happen if you did have that "ideal body?" How would your life be different? I've lost count of how many times I've heard women say, "When I reach my goal weight, then I'll..." or "Just 5 more pounds to go until I..." But it's interesting, I've never heard anyone arrive on the other side of that. I've never heard someone say "I'm so glad I went on that diet. If it weren't for that diet I'd never have..." Gone to the reunion? Met your husband? Gotten the job? I wonder, how do our bodies hold us back?

Typically, they don't unless you're dealing with a major health problem. However, living in our culture you're taught that your weight IS a problem. Something about YOU is out of control and you need to get it together so you can fit into an airplane seat just like the rest of us!* (Although many of us feel challenged to do that nowadays, and it's not our bodies, it's the very small seats!) Here's the challenge: it's our *perception* of our bodies that hold us back from our dreams-or even just being ourselves. Assuming of course your perception is negative. We can all identify with this, for haven't we all asked someone we loved, "does this make me look fat?" We're worried and assuming the worst.

In this case, perception is based on two things: early learning of what beautiful is, and the comparison dynamic. While I was growing up, I remember that beauty was mostly about being thin. You were somehow more successful being female if you were smaller. If you had problems with school, work, or relationships, it could possibly be due to how fat you were! I don't know what came first in that reasoning, but the scrutiny dynamic makes it hard to love yourself for sure! Growing up in an environment where everyone is sizing each other up encourages constant comparison. Today beauty is still about being thin, but it's also about objectifying yourself, being the right combination of sexy and innocent, and minimizing your power by keeping your mouth shut and your outer beauty as #1. That's not pretty, is it? And how in the world do we live up to these expectations anyway?

Comparison limits your ability to see beauty in yourself and in others. When you compare yourself to others, you end up either in a place of arrogance or despair. Neither of these emotional states gives you spiritual integrity. Both situations can lead to isolation and a lack of authenticity with yourself or others. Our comparisons can fuel obsessions about our bodies and their need to measure up. It's a vicious cycle that wears you out and only pretends to give you power. If pursuing the body of your dreams is costing you peace, isn't it worth reconsidering your approach?

Perhaps you have been on a health journey that involved restricting foods and changing the way you ate. There were diet rules in place, and you participated with a supportive group of friends. You've lost weight and feel more energetic. You've even felt more positive, in control, and confident about yourself. So maybe you are glad you went on that diet and you're reluctant to consider this perspective. Allow me to validate you on your choice to act on your own behalf! To me, you started to notice not just how the culture made you feel but how you were feeling in your skin. You resolved to do something about it. I think it's a great idea to look at what you're eating and evaluate how it makes you feel. "Intuitive Eating"[2] is a book that I use a lot, personally and professionally that encourages this. However, our culture offers a lot of confusing messages about food that I will get into this week. And one major LIE they perpetrate is that healthy=thin. You'll even be validated from friends when they say, "You look great, have you lost weight?" meaning the only way you look good is to be smaller. Sister, this is a LIE. I see this over and over again, where women make positive and healthy changes in their food plan and start exercising. But when they lose the excess weight and find their healthy weight, they're still not happy. They've made the physical changes but didn't realize that there are also emotional and spiritual implications to hating our bodies. And don't forget the cultural influence…geez this is can be complicated and emotional! But the truth is SIMPLE…you are lovely just the way you are. This must be embraced day to day even if you're on a weight loss plan.

Beauty: Galatians 5:24-25 "Those who belong to Christ Jesus have crucified the sinful nature with its passions and desires. Since we live by the Spirit, let us keep in step with the Spirit."

Bravery:
Day 1: You are a fascinating woman with a great story, I'm sure. Let's dig a bit, shall we? But first, take a few deep breaths. Check in with how you feel right now, both physically and then emotionally.

_____

_____

_____

Looking back on your life, what did you learn about beauty? How did the women in your family talk about their bodies? Share your answers with others if you're doing this in a group. Usually there's some humor and good stories here!

_____

_____

_____

_____

_____

_____

If God Himself taught you what beauty was, from the very beginning, how different do you think your life would be? Take a few minutes here, with your deep breathing and little to no distractions and imagine. Record your thoughts.

_____
_____
_____
_____
_____
_____

What affirming messages about beauty did you need to hear back then that would've made a difference today? Write them down and say them out loud and see how that feels.

_____
_____
_____
_____
_____
_____

What young girls are in your life now where you can make a difference and be a real body positive leader? Let the Spirit bring some names to you and write them down.

_____
_____
_____

Record an affirmative statement about yourself below. You could say, "I am a smart woman," "I'm brave to be asking deep questions like this," or simply "I am beautiful."

_____
_____
_____
_____

Day 2: You are a thoughtful, brave, and wise woman. With this affirmation, take a few deep breaths. Check in with how you feel right now, both physically and then emotionally.

_____

_____

_____

Alright, let's discuss the white elephant. How is wanting to lose weight such a bad thing? Am I really associating this with the "sinful nature" that needs to be crucified with its "passions and desires?" Um, well, for the most part, yeah. I am.

Sister, there are numerous ways we've been deceived and confused on what healthy is, the best way to get there, and what it looks like. The simple truth is that we all have a *physical heritage*. We've inherited the body types of our parents, our grandparents, and all the people that have come before them. We are meant to appear diverse. What looks healthy for one body type might look overweight to another. We can no longer judge by appearance but instead acknowledge that God reveals his beauty and yes, humor, in the diversity of body types all around us.

Instead of obsessing over a number or other comparisons, why not try this approach with your lifestyle goals:

- Be able to go where one wants to go
- Be able to do what one wants to do
- Have the energy to go where you want to go and do what you want to do
- Have a good bill of health

This philosophy[3] is conducive to loving how you feel in your skin. It works for every stage in your life. It gives you freedom to move your body and not be subject to burning or counting calories.

When I was first introduced to these guidelines a story came along with it. And yes, it's about weight loss. This particular person was a 3rd grade teacher who had a room full of students. Like many classrooms, she had lined up her kids in their desks in 4 rows. She often walked up and down these rows teaching and interacting with the children. Through the years this was her style, until she noticed something about her body that made it uncomfortable to walk up and down the rows. Her hips were starting to nudge the desks as she walked by. She was no longer able to do what she wanted to do. She could do it, but was uncomfortable about it. Who wouldn't be?

I like this simple story because our culture wasn't telling her to be smaller, it was her own experience that brought about a reality check, that maybe she needed to be more intentional over her food choices. I've been diet free for many years now, but I learned that from my last experience with restriction. It wasn't that I needed to be on a diet, it's that I just wasn't eating enough fruit and vegetables! And I was comforting myself with food too often instead of in with my emotions and figuring out what I really needed.

This may bring up some controversial and confusing feelings. We've all made choices about our food intake and may even feel defensive about them. You certainly owe no one an explanation over why you made these choices, and yet... be gentle with yourself and wonder...do I accept my physical heritage? Can I accept these simple lifestyle goals? Take at least 5 minutes to think through them, write down your thoughts, or talk with a friend.

_____
_____
_____
_____
_____
_____

Record an affirmative statement about yourself below. You can say, "My beauty is my physical heritage," "My body is healthy and strong," or "My beauty is my belly."

_____
_____
_____

Day 3: Hello Beautiful! Take a few deep breaths. There was a lot to think about yesterday. I want to be gentler today and give you more time to process. Check in with how you feel right now, both physically and then emotionally.

_____
_____
_____

While we are meant to be good stewards of our bodies, this doesn't mean that we need to take drastic measures with restricting our food choices. Today, people live "lifestyles" (as opposed to diets) reflecting a sense of morality or even cleanliness ("Clean" eating, anyone?). Cleanliness is next to godliness, right?? (Alison's answer: NO, and by the way that's not in the Bible.)

I'm about to ask you a lot of questions. Remember some important guidelines…be kind and don't judge yourself, be curious about your actions, and don't be afraid to act on your own behalf. Here we go.

How have you felt about your body in the past year? How much time have you used up feeling this way? Did you make any harsh choices for yourself based on feeling ashamed about your body? Did you feel this was living by the Spirit and keeping in step with the Spirit? Record your thoughts.

_____
_____
_____
_____
_____
_____
_____

Are there any rigid rules that God may want you to get rid of? Does this kind of freedom scare you? That would be normal. I often hear a common fear from women of ALL body types and it sounds like this…"If I give up my rules for the sake of loving my body, I will no longer have a body that I want to love." This horrendous lie, based in fear, is very hard to overcome. However you got to this point, it's extremely important to keep going and challenge this thought. Perhaps there could be something greater for you than the truth you believe this statement holds? Discuss your feelings and thoughts and record them.

_____
_____
_____
_____
_____
_____
_____
_____

Record an affirmative statement about yourself in your journal. You could say, "I belong to Jesus," "I will not be afraid," or "God wants me to love my body, therefore I will love my body."

_____
_____

Day 4: Take a few deep breaths. Check in with how you feel right now, both physically and then emotionally.

_____
_____
_____

It's often hard to challenge our body image and food choices because they're so personal to us. They serve some sort of function and to sacrifice this too seems like asking for too much. But look what you're swapping them out for! It's a leap to be sure, but one worth taking. This week I've asked you to look at Galatians 5:24-26. Here's "The Message"[4] version:

⟡

"Among those who belong to Christ, everything connected to getting our own way and mindlessly responding to what everyone else calls necessities is killed off for good-crucified. Since this is the kind of life we have chosen, the life of the Spirit, let us make sure that we do not just hold it as an idea in our heads or a sentiment in our hearts, but work out its implications in every detail of our lives. That means we will not compare ourselves with each other as if one of us were better and another worse. We have far more interesting things to do with our lives. Each of us is an original."

⟡

Read this over 5 times, each time pausing and breathing, allowing the Spirit to come in and draw your attention to a particular phrase. Write down the phrase and what you're feeling. Why do you think He drew your attention to this phrase? Listen, pray, and spend some time with your Father.

Phrase:_____

_____

_____

_____

Feelings/Thoughts:_____

_____

_____

_____

Record an affirming statement about yourself in your journal. You're on your own for this one. Hopefully God gave you a statement that will inspire you!

_____

_____

_____

Day 5: Hey there, Pretty Lady! Sit your beautiful- self down and let's breath. Check in with how you feel right now, both physically and then emotionally.

_____

_____

_____

I wonder how awesome our body image is going to be in the new heavens and new earth?! I believe we can have some of that now. Comparison is a natural dynamic that occurs in our minds, often without thinking about it. We want to belong in both comfortable and in unfamiliar surroundings. We just want to know we're o.k. and safe from rejection. When we're comparing, we're acting as if we don't belong to God, and He doesn't have our best interest at heart. We approach life like we have to do it by ourselves. To embrace being dearly loved, you must let go of what the world says your body should be, and instead name and claim your beauty.

Weekly Wrap-Up:

1. My body image is stronger this week because…

_____

_____

_____

_____

2. The issues that came up for me this week are:

    _____
    _____
    _____
    _____

3. What I did to seek understanding: (ie pray, talk to a friend, read a body image book)

    _____
    _____
    _____
    _____

4. What did I learn about myself this week?

    _____
    _____
    _____
    _____

5. What did I learn about God this week?

    _____
    _____
    _____
    _____

6. Look at Galatians 1:10. What does our culture expect from women in order to be "pleased?" What does God expect? Now look at Micah 6:8, from the Message: *"But He's already made it plain how to live, what to do, what God is looking for in men and women. It's quite simple: Do what is fair and just to your neighbor, be compassionate and loyal in your love, and don't take yourself too seriously-take God seriously."* Take a moment and write down what this verse means to you.

    _____
    _____
    _____
    _____

"The power of the feminine within God's image is FIERCE...yet we give it away freely when all we think about is how fat we are!!"

Week 4

Body: Reclaiming Dignity

I come from a long line of strong women. We are outspoken, funny, and have creative ideas. We're not afraid to try something new...as I'm writing I'm recalling a story about my Grandmother Marie, who took it upon herself to sell vitamins door to door in the 1950's. While the extra money was good for her family, she really chose to do this because she was passionate about her beliefs in alternative medicine. Pretty quickly though, in her small town of Greenville, SC, word got around that she was dabbling in witchcraft, just because she was selling vitamins.

My Mom was pretty gutsy too. She flew the coop and became a flight attendant for TWA in the 60's and lived in Manhattan with a half dozen other women in a small apartment (aka the "stew zoo"). While this was a fun job to have, you also had to weigh in before each flight. A 2002 article from Vanity Fair reports, "Supervisors routinely gave 'girdle checks,' a procedure that consisted of flicking an index finger against a buttock. Perceptible jiggle meant failure-and a possible suspension.[5]" With this kind of constant scrutiny, she and her friends got in the habit of starving themselves days before a job, then pigged out on first class meals once they were in the air. While that was just a short time in her life, it's been difficult to shed the "virtue" of skipping meals and eating super small portions to be beautiful.

I never really thought about how much this affected me. No one ever taught good body image practices. The only dynamic that gets handed down to girls is a standard of beauty defined by culture and crazy family ideas. I had a bad body image and my pursuit of health looked normal… diet pills, laxatives, over exercise, skipping meals, and body shaming myself and others.

But one day I had a daughter. Taking her for a grand visit to see all the ladies in my family, I loved sharing her, my pride and joy. I will never forget though my Aunt proclaiming how fat my girl was, as if it was a little too much. The rudeness of what I had tolerated and lived with hit me smack in the face. Today, this same girl stands at 5'8" and there's a reason she was in the 90th percentile besides good health…she was designed to be this way! Like God has a plan for our lives, He also has a plan for our bodies.

It's these moments that God brings us to that gives a challenge to previous assumptions that we had been living by. They are clues that our identity is based on something so much bigger than what our culture wants to limit it to. The power of the feminine within God's image is FIERCE…yet we give it away freely when all we think about is how fat we are!!

One of my favorite quotes is from Sue Monk Kidd, a very well- known author and speaker. She says, "That's the secret intent of life, of God—to move us continuously toward growth, toward recovering all that is lost and orphaned within us and restoring the divine image imprinted on our soul."[6]

In this journey, what is God reclaiming and restoring in you?

Beauty: I Timothy 4:7 "Have nothing to do with godless myths and old wives' tales, rather, train yourself to be godly."

Bravery:
Day 1: Hello, Beautiful and Important Lady! Take a few deep breaths. Check in with how you feel right now, both physically and then emotionally.

_____

_____

_____

_____

What thoughts or memories about your Mom come up for you? While it's easy to remember the negative ideas passed on, let's not forget the positive. There's probably something good that you could hold onto and pass on to future generations. If you're in a group, this is a great question for everyone to share something on, especially if it's positive. Let's not forget the influence of fathers either! Identify some of those times that helped, or maybe there are things that you wished you had heard from your Dad.

_____

_____

_____

_____

_____

_____

_____

Identify the "Godly" ideas to hold onto below. And of course, record an affirmative statement about yourself too.

_____

_____

_____

_____

Day 2: How's it going, Beauty Queen? Let's go just a little deeper today. Take a few deep breaths. Check in with how you feel right now, both physically and then emotionally.

_____

_____

_____

What do you think about the words "physical heritage?" What images come up for you? While everyone always tells me that I look just like my Mom, I feel that I represent my Dad's side a lot too. I can identify different physical traits that reflect the genetic path that I'm on. Some of these things honestly aren't great or culturally considered beautiful. I used to judge some of these things pretty harshly when I practiced body negativity. Judging them gave me a feeling of control, that perhaps if I worked hard enough these things wouldn't bother me anymore. It's taken a long time, but my harsh judgements no longer have much power over me. I see them for what they are...distractions from what's really going on in my life. I was losing opportunities to practice authenticity because there was a lack of confidence. When I see through all my self-criticism, I'm now observing a greater context in which it was all created. The culture, my family, my choices...NOW I can wonder about these thoughts that showed up. What was happening around me when I first started feeling this way? How do I feel about what was happening? And that's how loving your body works-getting through the negative body image and wondering what it's really all about.

Geneen Roth, author, speaker, and woman in recovery from her eating disorder, she advocates for 3 important rules when thinking about ourselves: 1) be kind, 2) be curious, and 3) be willing to act on your own behalf.[7] Every time negative body thoughts come up for you, they could be just that-a momentary distraction. But maybe it's something deeper... so let it be a red flag that you need to stop and be mindful because something's going on in your heart. Make the body shame work for you, instead of being a slave to it.

Was there a time you felt ashamed about your body? Is there a particular memory where someone's "sizeist" (someone who discriminates another based on their size)[8] attitude influenced how you felt about yourself? Record a body shame moment in your life.

_____

_____

_____

_____

After thinking of that moment, practice some self-care and write something about your physical heritage that you love. This will be your affirmative statement.

_____

_____

_____

_____

Day 3: Hello, Beautiful, Unique Lady! Get ready, we are going to POWER UP today! No red heels required. Take a few deep breaths, and feel free to stand like a superhero.[9] Check in with how you feel right now, both physically and then emotionally.

_____

_____

_____

Feminine Power. What images do those two words bring up for you? Burning bras, angry women, power hungry and ambitious girls-always wanting more and not caring who they step on to get it maybe? Timothy Leary, an American Psychologist and Writer said, "Women who seek to be equal with men lack ambition,"[10] which indicates that not only should we strive for equality, we can do even better.

Forget gender roles for this. Let's just talk about this phrase: "The power of the feminine within God's image is FIERCE…yet we give it away freely when all we think about is how fat we are!!" I think it's important for us to break this down a bit. What are some feminine characteristics? (gentleness, passionate, receptive, intuitive, compassionate, family oriented to name a few). Can you think of times when God reveals these characteristics in Himself? What does that tell you about Him?

_____

_____

_____

He's also a Strong, Bold Provider. He's ambitious in His creation and is our Ultimate Authority. But that authority becomes more inviting when the feminine is embraced-His loving, dedicated, passionate yet strong place of God the Father in our lives. What happens when we put something between us? He gets jealous. He said it himself, "I am jealous God" (Exodus 20:5).

Our world tells you to put all your power into your outer beauty. That's success-if you're pretty you get stuff and people like you. You don't even have to know God personally to know how terrible this is. Yet we play these games to some extent when we let body shame take us away from our lives.

What would that look like for you to reclaim some power? The Scripture from this week says to "train yourself to be godly." What would it be like to include the feminine in this description? Imagine and meditate on this throughout the day. Ask God to show you, and promise to listen. Write down any personal insights gained below:

_____

_____

_____

And don't forget...write another affirmative statement about yourself below. You could say, "My feminine voice is important to my God," or "I am brave and strong," or "My compassion and gentleness are powerful tools in God's eyes."

_____

_____

_____

Day 4: You Fierce Warrior! Take a few deep breaths. Check in with how you feel right now, both physically and then emotionally.

_____

_____

_____

"Train yourself to be godly." This is a pretty simple verse to meditate on and memorize this week. I love the simple ones because sometimes they are the most profound. Breaking them down can bring so much meaning to any given moment.

I'm focusing on the word "train." This word reflects consistent work, daily or several times a week at least, with a working goal in mind. What is your goal? Here, it's to have a better body image, which is why we practice at least 5 times weekly. Hopefully it's on your mind as well on your "off" days.

How is your training going? You know, we're almost done. There's only one more week to go. Have you been taking this seriously, or just doing it for someone else? Sometimes we hide behind good things to manipulate others. If they think we're doing the right thing, we can hide deeper into ourselves and get away with murder.

Be authentic. Whether you're choosing a myth or a reformed, healthy-self path, be honest. Tell someone. You are loved either way.

Record an affirmative statement about yourself in your journal. You could say, "No matter what, I am loved by God."

_____

_____

_____

Day 5: Hey Sweet Lady! You are on the last day of this week! Take a moment to pat yourself on the back for this accomplishment. One more week left, and already you've done so much work. You are amazing! Now, let's breathe. Check in with how you feel right now, both physically and then emotionally.

_____

_____

_____

I have an idea...reclaim your dignity and power. Sounds good but how in the heck do you do that?? Here, we need to re-focus your mindset.

It's easier to follow through on the details if you've got the proper motivation and an openness to change the dynamics and decisions that hold you back.

So I'm ending this week with a practical application to add to your training experience. Several years ago when I first started the Body, Beauty, and Bravery Project™, I was still figuring myself out. I had the opportunity to speak to several different types of audiences over the first couple of years and it really challenged me. Every time I had a presentation I had to search my heart and ask what the audience in particular needed to hear from me. What would be especially helpful, challenging, and empowering?

Finally, I came up with my own personal list of what's helpful, challenging, and ultimately empowering to me. I still have this, and plan to never throw this piece of paper away! Here are a few things on my list:

1. No numbers: I will not weigh myself outside of the doctor's office. When I do go there and get on the scale, I remind myself that it's just a number. This number will give me feedback on where the healthy set weight of my body may be. It will also tell me if my thyroid meds are working. And I promise myself not to change my plans for any meals or snacks that day no matter what the number is. In fact, I plan the menu ahead of time so all the food is bought and ready to go. My number is just a number.

2. Time with my girls: spending time together and figuring out what's important in the lives of each one is a full time job. I really love knowing them though, and our inside jokes that we create together are priceless. I can smile even when I feel overwhelmed.

3. Practicing what I preach: I really do believe in intuitive eating. I teach this to my girls and we usually have an "open pantry" policy. If someone can't figure out what to have as a snack, we have a dialogue that they later learn to do themselves. Have you had any fruits or vegetables yet today? Then grab one of those food groups, add a carb or a protein and there you go. We enjoy a

variety of foods, I teach my girls to cook, and there's no body shame in my house. No one has to clean their plate. Knowing you're satisfied is a skill we learn to pay attention to.

Other things include my faith, my significant other, exercise…I wish I could see everyone's list. Spend some thoughtful time on this and record it below.

_____
_____
_____
_____
_____
_____
_____
_____

Weekly wrap up:

1. My body image is better this week because…

_____
_____
_____

2. The issues that came up for me this week are:

_____
_____
_____

3. What I did to seek understanding: (ie pray, talk to a friend, read a body image book)

_____
_____
_____

4. What did I learn about myself this week?

_____

_____

_____

_____

5. What did I learn about God this week?

_____

_____

_____

_____

6. Jesus reflected the value that women have in the way He spoke to them. Often He chose to speak to the kind of woman no one would be caught dead talking to. Take a look at a few of these Scriptures:
    *   John 4:1-30
    *   John 8:1-11
    *   Mark 5:21-43

    As you read these passages, try reading them in a different versions and compare the language. What stands out to you that's especially tender? Do you envision Jesus talking to you like that? What would He say to you now, knowing that you're working on having a better body image?

_____

_____

_____

_____

_____

_____

_____

"Keep fighting to use your voice...be brave."

Week 5

Body: My Authentic Beauty, My Authentic Voice

Sister, we've covered so much so far in this series! We've talked about:

1. My body image
2. Media and Cultural ideas of beauty
3. My body image (again)
4. Playing the victim
5. Comparison
6. My Family
7. What Empowers Me

And that doesn't include all the exercises! Hopefully all of this is starting something new in you. Do you feel it? Do you feel your own story beginning to emerge? Hoping those paradigms are shifting big time and you're feeling hopeful. When God works in our lives, His light shines through the thick blanket of worthlessness that Satan likes to cover us with.

I notice that when I'm having a negative body image moment that it seems to connect with other problems in my life that don't seem to have an easy (or any) solution. Part of my journey was realizing these moments for what they are. In some ways this physical focus is a distraction-a way to deal. If I'm hung up about weight or a specific body part, I can do things to work on that. I have that power. And while oppressive, it also feels a bit familiar and resolvable. This is a lot easier to tolerate than actually putting a voice and feelings to my problems.

Or is it?

When I realized the problem wasn't my body, then I had the task of tuning into my environment, listening to the physical reactions my body was having, and giving myself time and space to figure out how I felt. Then maybe I could share myself, my soul with those around me. I'm not sure that this process of finding the authentic voice ever ends.

But I do feel more genuine and real, like my friends and family are finally getting a glimpse of the real me. This isn't always comfortable...or safe...but it's authentic.

I feel free.

Beauty: Galatians 5:1 "It is for freedom that Christ has set us free. Stand firm, then, and do not let yourselves be burdened again by a yoke of slavery."

English Standard Version "...and do not submit again to a yoke of slavery."

The Message "Christ has set us free to live a free life. So take your stand! Never again let anyone put a harness of slavery on you. (vs 2) I am emphatic about this."

Bravery:

Day 1: Good day, Authentic Beauty! Take a few deep breaths. Check in with how you feel right now, both physically and then emotionally.

_____

_____

_____

What does authentic beauty mean to you? What images come to mind? Take a few minutes to write down some thoughts. You can come back during the week and add to this.

_____

_____

_____

_____

How does this help you feel free? What will your authentic beauty require from you to stand firm and not be enslaved again?

_____
_____
_____
_____

Record an affirmative statement about yourself below. How about, "I am an Authentic Beauty."??

_____
_____
_____

Day 2: Hello Beautiful! Take a few deep breaths. Check in with how you feel right now, both physically and then emotionally.

_____
_____
_____

Was yesterday's assignment tough? When roadblocks come up it's usually because we don't regularly practice self-love. Matthew 27 says "Love your neighbor as you love yourself." Maybe we're not loving our neighbor enough because we're not tuned into the specific ways we need to practice self-love. I'm not talking about selfishness here, I'm talking about recognizing your value in the eyes of Christ. You are worthy to be loved and cherished.

Here's a reminder of what I've asked you to do in past weeks: When you see yourself in the mirror, instead of focusing on something negative, pick out something positive that you are grateful for. Find something about your genetic heritage that's beautiful. It's also helpful to think of yourself as a whole, human being and be grateful for what your body does for you daily. What about your inner traits? Are you determined, patient, or funny? What kind of person are you, and how do you show love and kindness for others? Affirm yourself for these as well-your heart is what God looks at and is after the most (I Samuel 16:7).

Record an affirmative statement about yourself in your journal. What makes you, you? List your traits as an affirmation, an acknowledgement of what makes you authentic.

_____

_____

_____

Day 3: Gorgeous Lady! Take a few deep breaths. Check in with how you feel right now, both physically and then emotionally.

_____

_____

_____

What does recovery from enslaving thoughts look like? How do we get to be emphatic about our freedom?

What keeps us locked up could be some early painful memories and comments that people who loved us were a part of. This can still hurt very deeply. These experiences often lead to feelings of rejection and beliefs that we're not worthy somehow. They are deadly seeds that are planted and have potential to grow into something massive. Our minds become enslaved which then affects our actions.

Do these thoughts bring up something specific? Let's change what happened, shall we? Now, in this moment, you are a dearly loved child, a fierce woman of God who loves herself, and in possession of wisdom... You walk right up to your child self, stuck in a moment where you've just been teased, bullied, or harmed in some way and say...

"_____!" (You fill in the blank).

Just because you couldn't use your voice in the moment then, or in moments now, doesn't mean you're not here, beautiful, and worthy to listen to. Keep fighting to use your voice...be brave.

Let your statement above be your affirmation statement today. Ponder it, and let it be something you tell yourself again and again, beyond this day.

_____
_____
_____

Day 4: My dear Sister in Christ! You are so wise to take some time today to practice self-love. Let's breathe. Check in with how you feel right now, both physically and then emotionally.

_____
_____
_____

"I am emphatic about this."
What are your passions in life? Feeling comfortable in your skin is a practical skill. What would it be like to practice this in your passion? Would you be more like yourself? Or maybe more playful? Are there ways self-doubt could be holding you back? What have you not done or said because you felt self-conscious?

_____
_____
_____
_____

Are you being called to claim freedom in other areas of your life? Record your thoughts on this, and of course, write down an affirmative statement about yourself in your journal.

_____
_____
_____
_____

Day 5: Dearly Loved Child, you have arrived! I am so proud of you. Take a few deep breaths. Check in with how you feel right now, both physically and then emotionally.

_____

_____

_____

Imagine yourself 5 weeks ago…what did it feel like to begin this study? What were your reservations, or what scared you the most?

_____

_____

_____

_____

What are you the most proud of?

_____

_____

_____

_____

What are some things you'd like to continue to work on?

_____

_____

_____

_____

How will you go about working on these things?

_____

_____

_____

_____

Weekly wrap up:

1. How I feel about my body now has changed in the following ways...

   _____
   _____
   _____
   _____

2. The issues that came up for me this week are:

   _____
   _____
   _____
   _____

3. What I did to seek understanding: (ie pray, talk to a friend, read a body image book)

   _____
   _____
   _____

4. What did I learn about myself this week?

   _____
   _____
   _____

5. What did I learn about God this week?

   _____
   _____
   _____

6. If you're in a group, share your answers from the week. What does Authentic Beauty mean to you? How did you practice self-love this week? What was your affirmation statement from day 3? How have you held back in the past, and in what ways do you see yourself emerging?

7. Group idea: Everyone has a bag or a box with their name on it. Have each member write something positive about each and every person. Then drop those comments in everyone's bag. Take turns and go around, with each member reading their positive comments out loud.

Concluding Thoughts

Dear Sister,

Thank you so much for choosing this five-week journey. There are many forces at play that influence our decisions. The circumstances of our lives and the placement of where we're at in the world also affects where we focus our attention. My point is, something brought you to this book, this experience, and I'm grateful that you invested your time and energy. I'm most grateful to the God that orchestrates our lives and brought you to this place.

This journey of learning to love ourselves and being comfortable in our own skin can take a very long time! But the older I get I'm starting to realize that maybe this is one of the major ongoing experiences in life. We all have our own purpose and passions, which means we're striving in some way daily. But it's a redemptive journey like this that causes us to slow down and take in the significance we have in Christ. We can never just take this acceptance in because it's so foreign and unnatural! We didn't do anything to deserve this but we have it anyway. What a beautiful gift.

Such radical love this is, and I hope that you always feel His presence and realize that you are and always will be His dearly loved child. For more inspirational connections, or to know more about the Body, Beauty, and Bravery Project, check out my website

at www.bodybeautybravery.com or follow me on Facebook on my page, Body, Beauty, & Bravery.
Live beautiful, live brave!
Love,
Alison

References

1. "Killing Us Softly, Part 4" by Jean Kilbourne is part of a documentary series that's been changing lives all over the world by bringing attention to how women are portrayed in advertising.

2. "Intuitive Eating" by Evelyn Tribole, MS, RD, and Elyse Resch, MS, RDN, CEDRD. This wonderful book is something I use personally and professionally. There's a more child friendly version now, as well as a workbook. Like many of my favorites, it's covered in coffee stains and well worn! Very practical and liberating read.

3. "Be able to go where one wants to go, be able to do what one wants to do, have the energy to go where you want to go and do what you want to do, have a good bill of health." This philosophy is not mine originally. An old friend shared her notes from a workshop she attended entitled "Slim for Him," which was a workshop calling Christians to be accountable for connecting slimness with pleasing God. These guidelines were in those notes but the author's name was not on the presentation notes I received. Despite searching, her name is still a mystery to me.

4. "The Message: the Bible in Contemporary Language" by Eugene H. Peterson.

5. http://www.vanityfair.com/news/2002/10/stewardesses-golden-era

6. Sue Monk Kidd is a writer and speaker from Sylvestor, GA. She's best known for her book, "The Secret Life of Bees," but I'm a huge

fan of her written personal journey in "Dance of the Dissident Daughter."

7. "When You Eat at the Refrigerator, Pull Up a Chair: 50 Ways to Feel Thin, Gorgeous, and Happy (When You Feel Anything But)" by Geneen Roth.

8. The definition of "sizeist" came from Wikipedia.org. When I speak to kids on body image, I introduce this term to them. For further education on a worldwide movement that's taking this message further, check out www.haescommunity.com (Health at Every Size).

9. Stand Like a Superhero! Hear more about this whole concept at: https://www.ted.com/talks/amy_cuddy_your_body_language_shapes_who_you_are#t-114535

10. Timothy Francis Leary gave us this wonderful quote about women. In addition to being a writer and psychologist, he was also known for embracing the countercultural movement of the 1960's and was "an advocate of psychedelic drug research and use." Well, it wasn't like I could quote Martin Luther! http://www.goodreads.com/author/show/47718.Timothy_Leary

About the Author

Hi there! Here's a little about me...I am a bit of a free spirit and had no clue what I wanted to do at 18, but Psychology sounded the most interesting so I went for it. I attended Covenant College on top of Lookout Mtn, GA. and loved the journey! My direction in life became clearer as I thrived from that literal mountain top experience.

After a couple of years obtaining "life experience" in Chattanooga, I left for the big city, aka Atlanta to attend Richmont Graduate University and Georgia State to obtain dual degrees in Christian Counseling and an MS in Community Counseling. Since then I've worked in various settings serving women and girls recovering from Eating Disorders in the Atlanta area, including the Atlanta Center for Eating Disorders, Ridgeview Institute, and currently, the Center for Discovery.

For the past 5 years I've been in a group practice at the Atlanta Counseling Center and seeing a variety of clients on an outpatient basis. I'm a very down to earth person, and I love what I do. I enjoy being present with my client as he or she talks about whatever they're dealing with lately. I usually work with eating disorders, body image issues, binge eating, depression, anxiety, trauma, addiction, grief, and coping with life changes. I use a variety of theoretical approaches to help whomever comes into the room to reduce whatever stress they're feeling. Humor also tends to show up.

I'm also known for my work with the Body, Beauty, & Bravery Project™. This is a program I started back in 2007 to help empower women and girls to feel comfortable in their own skin. I've been leading camps for girls 9-12 years old teaching them some of these very same concepts discussed in this book! Looking to the future, B3P will be looking at innovative ways to include boys into the conversation and workshops. Stay connected if you like at www.bodybeautybravery.com.

When I'm not busy with all of these great things, I'm spending time with my four beautiful girls, my incredible husband, and crazy dog.

Made in the USA
Columbia, SC
16 February 2019